The Complete Guide to Tarot Reading

Hali Morag

Since their appearance in the 14th century, Tarot cards have become a world-wide phenomenon. In recent years, their use has become widespread. Mystics and philosophers have developed Tarot reading on the theoretical level. Gypsies, in particular, have helped spread the practical use of Tarot cards for everyday purposes.

The Tarot pack comprises 78 cards divided into two systems, a primary system and a secondary one. Each card has its own meaning and its own mystical and numerological background used in interpretation. By dealing the cards and analyzing their layout it is possible to solve problems, predict the future, recognize previous incarnations, and receive answers to troubling problems.

Tarot reading is a serious, consistent, and logical system. After learning about the significance of the cards, we move on to various layouts and see how and what can be revealed using the hidden information in the cards.

In an easy and systematic way, this book enables readers to become familiar with Tarot cards and to use them for spiritual and everyday purposes.

Hali Morag was born to a family of Hungarian origin — a country where Gypsies became experts in the use of Tarot cards as an art and a trade. He learned Tarot reading from his mother and used this knowledge during his world travels to make a living by reading Tarot cards in mystical centers and for private clients. Hali is the author of guide books to Tarot reading and palmistry and lives alternately in Israel, India, and France.

ASTROLOG COMPLETE GUIDES SERIES

The Complete Guide to Coffee Grounds and Tea Leaf Reading
Sara Zed

The Complete Guide to Palmistry
Batia Shorek

The Complete Guide to Tarot Reading
Hali Morag

Crystals - Types, Use and Meaning
Connie Islin

The Dictionary of Dreams
Eili Goldberg

Meditation: The Journey to Your Inner World
Eidan Or

Playing Cards: Predicting Your Future
Hali Morag

Day-by-Day Numerology
Lia Robin

Using Astrology To Choose Your Partner
Amanda Starr

The I Ching
Nizan Weisman

The Complete Guide to
Tarot Reading

Hali Morag

Astrolog Publishing House

Astrolog Publishing House
P. O. Box 1123, Hod Hasharon 45111, Israel
Tel: 972-9-7412044
Fax: 972-9-7442714
E-Mail: info@astrolog.co.il
Astrolog Web Site: www.astrolog.co.il

ISBN 965-494-007-8

Published by Astrolog Publishing House 1999

Printed in Israel
10 9 8 7 6 5 4 3

CONTENTS

Introduction 7

The major Arcana 11

Interpreting the cards in the major Arcana 55

Before revealing the cards 83

The spreads 87

The minor Arcana 102

Cups 105

Wands 116

Pentacles 128

Swords 138

Knight 147

The numerology of the Tarot cards 150

The spreads 153

INTRODUCTION

The origin of cards in general, and tarot cards in particular, is not known for sure, and there are as many suppositions as there are researchers on the subject. Hand-drawn playing cards first appeared at the beginning of the 12th century, and these were based on the principles of the tarot cards we know today.

Tarot cards, which first appeared in the 14th century in northern Italy, are the earliest cards we know, and were used both for games and for mystical purposes; later on, the modern deck of tarot cards developed from these.

The deck of tarot cards is divided into two sets or arcanas — the Major Arcana and the Minor Arcana (or Lesser Arcana).

The Major Arcana is composed of 22 picture cards: 21 of these are numbered consecutively from 1 to 21, and there is also a un-numbered card or a card with the value of zero — known as The Fool. The 22 cards correspond to the 22 letters of the Hebrew alphabet.

There are small differences between different decks of cards, primarily relating to the location of The Fool, either at the beginning or the end of the deck, and the location of the cards numbered 8 and 11.

The Minor Arcana includes 56 cards, divided into four sets (suits) of 13 cards: Swords, Wands, Cups and

Pentacles; and four Knight cards. The Minor Arcana is the same in most types of tarot decks.

Tarot cards were used for games, to predict the future, and to study complex mystical knowledge. The Major Arcana represents a totally symbolic system, considered to be a key to the mysteries and knowledge of the true nature of man, the universe and God. We can discern Kabbalistic, Gnostic, neo-Platonic and other mystical influences that have contributed to the design of the symbols appearing on the face of the tarot cards.

There is also a theory that the cards originated in China or India, and that they were brought to Europe by Gypsies. According to another theory, the cards were transmitted to subsequent generations by Kabbalistic sages in the year 1200. And there are many practicing the occult arts who believe that tarot cards are the essence of ancient Egyptian knowledge.

Besides their use as a means for meditation, as well as mystical and magical guidance, tarot cards are used to foretell the future, in a broader and more extensive manner than the rules and methods governing fortune-telling using a an ordinary deck of cards (Playing cards).

There are many types of tarot cards. The most common, designed primarily for those first learning the method, are the Rider-Waite cards, samples of which are used in this book.

The act of predicting the future itself requires a great deal of intuition, imagination, diplomacy and tact; the different interpretations suggested for deciphering the cards should be used as a basis, which will guide you through your fortune-telling activities.

Take care not to abuse your card-reading ability. You must remember that you carry a great responsibility as a card-reader. People often take the future that is foretold them more seriously than they think.

If you find a **spread** (display of the cards) that foretells death, illness, betrayal, failure — try to describe this as tactfully and gently as possible. Remember that your interpretation could always be mistaken. Remember that there are several methods for interpreting tarot cards, but the basis for each method is to know the special meaning of each card.

When the tarot card is turned over facing up it may appear with its head facing the querent — the person who is seeking an answer from the cards, or the reader, when he has laid out a spread for himself — this card is called a **direct card**, or **"upright"** card, and is given its regular interpretation. When the card faces away from the querent, the card is called a **reverse card**, and its interpretation changes. This is important mostly in the cards of the first set, the Major Arcana, and less so in second, the Minor Arcana.

In this book you will find the foundations for a

complete understanding of tarot cards, according to the classic traditions which developed primarily in Europe. Take time to examine what is written on the cards, distinguish between the description of the card and its meaning in fortune-telling, practice dealing the cards... and you will be able to take a significant preliminary step towards becoming familiar with them.

THE MAJOR ARCANA

1 The Magician

THE MAGICIAN.

The image of a young man in a magician's robe, similar to the portrait of Apollo, bright-eyed and smiling a confident smile. Above his head is the mysterious symbol of the holy spirit, the symbol of life, a never-ending strand which creates a horizontal figure-eight: ∞. Around the magician's waist is a belt in the form of a snake, grasping its tail in its mouth. This snake is generally recognized as a symbol of eternity, and here it symbolizes the eternity of the spirit.

In his right hand the magician holds a wand, lifted towards the sky, while his left hand points towards the earth. This dual symbol (above/below) is well-known in mysticism, and indicates light, beauty and splendor that is obtained from the power from above, and its transmission to the material world below. Thus the magician controls the powers of the spirit.

On the table in front of the magician, there are four symbols from the tarot deck: a wand, a pentacle, a cup and a sword. These represent the four elements of nature that are placed before the magician, and he uses them as he wishes. Beneath the table are roses and lilies, a flowering garden which indicates divine inspiration. There are mystical symbols on the table, on the pentagram and in between the flowers. Part of the table is hidden, indicating that not everything is revealed before man. "There is more that is hidden than is revealed." Pay attention to the many lines that point upwards toward the heavens — the wand, the sleeves of the robe, the legs of the table, the base of the cup, and other lines as well.

This card represents the divine motive in man, the divine spark, the desire to unite with the supreme power. This is also the symbol of the unity of the individual found in all the arcanas. The connection with the number 8 which in Christianity is the symbol of life or renewed life, is obvious. And as everyone knows, the symbol for infinity is ∞ which rules the magician like a crown on his head.

2 The High Priestess

At the feet of the High Priestess lies the half crescent of the moon, and on her head is the crown of the "diadem" with horns, and the earth in its center, and the Cross of the Great Sun on her breast. The scroll in her hand bears the inscribed word "**Tora**" (Torah), representing eternal law, the great secret and the wisdom of the world. The scroll is partially covered by the robe of the High Priestess, indicating that part of her wisdom is hidden, while part is revealed. She sits between two columns, one black and one white, Boaz and Jachin, columns of the mystical temple, with the temple curtain behind her, embroidered with palm trees and pomegranates.

The High Priestess sits amidst flowers, and the picture hints at light, the realm of brilliance. The High Priestess is on the threshold of the Temple of Wisdom of Isis, Priestess of occult wisdom, as well as the Priestess of the Hidden Church, which unites God and man. She also represents "the second marriage" of the prince who is no longer of this world — she is the spiritual bride, the holy virgin, mother, daughter of the stars from the Garden of Eden above. She is the queen of borrowed light — of all the light! She is the moon nursing from the milk of the supreme mother.

In actuality, she is the reflection of the purity of the supreme mother, thus her name is "Shechina." According to the Kabbala, the Shechina exists above (and then her name is "Binah," understanding), and below (and then here name is "Malkhut," kingship). In mystical terms, the Shechina is the spiritual bride of the just man, who knows the law and wisdom of the universe. In certain cases, this card is the highest and most important card in the Major Arcana.

3 The Empress

THE EMPRESS.

The Empress is an impressive image, seated, wearing a robe, richly and royally dressed, daughter of heaven and earth. Her crown is composed of stars, forming the shape of a triangle. The sign of Venus is found on the shield resting at her feet. There is a field of wheat in front of her, and behind her appears a waterfall. The staff she holds in her hand is adorned with a miniature orb of the planet Earth. She is Heaven on earth, a terrestrial Garden of Eden, symbolizing the material world of man.

But she is not a "familiar queen" — she is still an exalted image, mother of all man, exalted above any "familiar queen." There are those who describe The

Empress as desire, and attach wings to her, as if she came from the light of the sun. This is the Queen of Nature, the goddess of the Earth (and under no circumstances is she an "angel," she is not a soul who was given "wings"!).

She is above all earthly things — this stems from the direct message man receives that he is born of woman, but she bears the implementation of this message, since she is above and beyond earthliness.

The card of the Empress symbolizes the idea of the gate through which we enter this world, the Garden of Venus. The secret of this path that leads beyond the gate is in the keeping of the High Priestess (card no. 2), so the Empress is the intermediary between the Priestess and the subject who calls upon her. But we must not look for a simple match between the Empress and the world, the divine nature or the Holy Trinity — the Empress is the gateway!

4 The Emperor

THE EMPEROR.

The Emperor sits on a throne, holding the world in his left hand like a ball. He is a crowned ruler — exalted, commanding, reigning from a raised throne whose armrests and back are engraved with the heads of goats. He is the one who takes action, who realizes the power of the world, and bears all the signs of that power.

He sits upon a throne that is solid and square (and sometimes he is portrayed as seated upon a cube of stone). He is a dynamic, driving force, to whom the Empress reacts, and in this sense we can say that he removes the curtain from upon the face of Isis (yet she still remains the "exalted woman," unchanged).

It is important to remember that the Emperor and the Empress (cards no. 3 and 4) are not married to each other, but this connection is hinted. On the surface, they are united upon the throne but beyond this there is an additional presence, even more important — they represent the Kingdom of Heaven, the spiritual throne. They control the spiritual throne and the material throne.

Often, the Emperor is described as representing the power of one's will, but remember that this in only one of his components. Under no circumstances should you associate the Emperor entirely with the absolute, the eternal.

5 The Hierophant

THE HIEROPHANT

The Hierophant wears a triangular crown and is seated between two columns, but these are not the columns of Jachin and Boaz, the columns in the temple of the High Priestess. In his left hand is a staff in the shape of the triple-cross, and in his right hand he is forming the famous sign of the priestly blessing in Judaism, an esoteric symbol which differentiates between the manifest Torah and the hidden Torah. It is important to note that the image of the High Priestess makes no signs.

At the feet of the Hierophant is a pair of crossed keys, and two "holy servants" are bowing before him (for this reason, the Hierophant is sometimes referred to as "The

Pope," a well-known image but which embodies only some of the symbolism of the Hierophant). He is the power that controls external religion, just as the High Priestess controls the exotic, covert religion.

The meaning of the card can change, within a wide range, from place to place. There are those who see the power of the card in the pair of keys, which open the gates of wisdom (the keys to heaven of Petros in Christianity).

It is clear that the Hierophant represents what is right and holy in the visible side of the world. As such, he is the link between the official, institutional world (in contrast with the natural world) and man, and leads the religious and spiritual salvation of the human race. He stands at the head of a religious order, and this order reflects a broader, divine harmony. And it is important to remember — even when the Hierophant forgets that he is only the head of a "reflective" order and acts as if he is everything and there is no one else besides him — that the Hierophant is not the divine authority.

The head of a theological order — yes. The essence of everything — no! Therefore, the difference between him and the Emperor is also clear.

6 The Lovers

THE LOVERS.

The sun shines in the sky above, and beneath is a large winged image whose arms are outstretched, protective, casting its influence below. On the ground are two figures, a man and a woman, naked like Adam and Eve in the Garden of Eden before they ate the apple. Behind the man is the Tree of Life, bearing a dozen fruit, and behind the women is the Tree of Knowledge, which differentiates between right and wrong, with the snake wrapped around it.

The figures are young, virginal, innocent and symbolize Love before it was corrupted by physical desire.

Simplistically, we can say that this card symbolizes

human love, which is presented as part of the way, the truth and the life. (This is preferable to presenting the card as purely a marriage card.) At the highest symbolic level, this card is related to the mysteries of the witches' gatherings, the coven and the Sabbath.

We must take note of the symbolism in the winged creature — it divides man from the sun, and intermediates between heaven and earth.

The image of the woman symbolizes the attraction towards an emotional life, the law of divine Providence. It is only through her that the man can arise above the earth and complete himself as a perfect essence. Thus, and there is no doubt about this, this card belongs to the female cards of mystery. And it is important to remember, this is the first card to have two human images.

7 The Chariot

THE CHARIOT.

This figure is standing erect, noble, decorated with symbols, carrying a drawn spear (or sword). On the shoulders of the figure are symbols from the Urim and Tummim (an oracle worn by the Jewish high priest in the Holy Temple, together with a tunic and breastplate).

The figure is leading towards victory. He triumphs and conquers on all planes — in the mind, in science, in progress. He faces the mysteries of the Sphinx, and as evidence of this, two images of the Sphinx are pulling the Chariot. First and foremost, despite the spear, he succeeds in the area of the mind.

The pair of Sphinx images, black and white, represents

the mysteries of nature (day/night, hot/cold), and the figure cannot supply them with an answer; the walls of the city, appearing behind the figure are evidence of battle plans and external victories, but not internal within the figure. The black and white, the Urim and Tummim, signify that the figure is bound by the rules of logic. He must drive the chariot without reins, through the power of his logic alone!

It is important to relate the size of the image and the height — it is obvious that if we compare the Chariot with the High Priestess, the chariot cannot "enter" the gate of the Priestess, and therefore, neither can the image be saved by the Torah scroll. He is incapable of answering the questions posed to him by the High Priestess. The figure is neither Emperor, king nor priest, and therefore, its connections to the previous six cards are "tenuous."

8 Strength

A woman, above whose head is floating the symbol we recognize from the card of "The Fool," is closing the jaws of the lion. In contrast with other drawings, in this card the lion has already been tamed, indicated by the wreath of flowers around the lion's neck.

Frequently, card no. 8 in the Major Arcana is the card of "Justice" (which appears in this list as card no. 11). In actuality, there is no great significance to this. The fact the here it is the eighth card, stems from the natural development of the images so far. The wreath of flowers represents the plow, the yoke that is easy to bear, of divine law, when it comes from the heart (and then it is not a burden, but rather a support!). Thus the earthly woman, whose symbol of the infinite goes with her (recognition of divine law), can control the king of beasts without difficulty.

This card has no relation to self-confidence in the usually accepted way, rather it symbolizes the power of those whose strength is hidden within their belief in God, who dwells in their heart.

There are those who claim that the lion signifies desire, and the one called "strength" has the divine power to free herself from the control of her desires (similar to: "Who is strong? He who conquers his will."). This strength enables the figure to subdue the lion as if it were a kitten.

It is important to notice that this is the first card with the appearance of an attribute — Strength — rather than an image, necessarily (although the attributes are expressed through images, as actors).

9 The Hermit

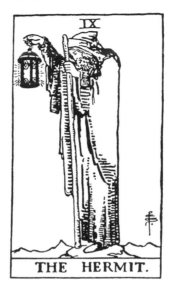

THE HERMIT.

The figure of the hermit in this series of cards is characterized by the lantern, which is totally visible. Inside the lantern a star is shining, and thus the two ideas are connected — antiquity and the light of the world.

Regarding the mystical and esoteric nature of the card, there are many interpretations: The wise man who is searching, with the help of the light from the "star," for truth and justice (and therefore, Justice cannot be the eighth card, since the wise man has not yet found it).

There are those who interpret the Hermit as searching for truth and justice within himself, since his head is bent down toward his heart.

The long staff in his hand hints that the journey to find truth and justice is a long and tedious one (or the staff, which is the same height as the Hermit, tells us that this journey will take the person's entire life).

10 The Wheel of Fortune

The Wheel of Fortune, or the Wheel of Fate, is the first card on which there is no real image of a person, only mystical images and symbols. The symbols appearing on this card are primarily from Egyptian and Kabbalistic origin. It is important to note that the image of the angel on the card is not the figure of a person, rather the figure of an angel! The images of the cherubs appearing in the corners of the card — the lion, the ram, the eagle and the man — symbolize the images found in the vision of Ezekiel (or the vision of John in Christianity), and they are taken from the Jewish Kabbala. Around the wheel there are three figures — Typhon in the form of a snake; Anubis, a figure whose upper half is in the form of a jackal and whose lower half is the form of a man, leading the souls of the dead to the grave; and the Sworded Sphinx. Within the wheel are four symbols taken from alchemy, the elements of fire, earth, water and air, with the symbols for mercury, sulfur, water and salt. The four Latin letters on the wheel, spell out "TORA" (Torah), TARO (tarot) and ROTA (that is, wheel). Notice that every image, in addition to its symbolism, also illustrates an action, such as the angels who are reading their books, for example. And of course, the Tetragrammaton, God's Ineffable name, the letters (in Hebrew) ה ו ה י , etched within the wheel. The Wheel of Fortune card is found in balance through perpetual motion, with the Sphinx acting as the balance of the wheel. The wheel represents the idea of stability through movement.

The number four is repeated throughout the card: the 4 cherubs of Ezekiel, 4 elements, 4 letters in God's name, 4 Latin letters, 4 symbols of alchemy; 4 is also a number which symbolizes cycles, such as the four seasons. Only the three symbols of Egyptian origin balance the movement of four. And the numbers 3 and 4, in reality, summarize the entire tarot system.

This card, with its multiple symbols, actually presents the complete tarot system. Occasionally, it is enough to analyze this card very carefully in order to understand the entire system, in terms of its mysticism and esoteric meaning (but not for the purposes of fortune-telling and interpretation!).

11 Justice

This card bears all the familiar symbols associated with "justice" — the scales symbolizing equilibrium, the sword symbolizing wisdom as expressed through justice, the two pillars representing good and evil, the crown that bestows authority. To a certain extent, this is a transfer of the power of the high priestess into the hands of man.

It is important to understand the meaning of the two columns and the curtain, which embellish the figure, indicating the moral principle according to which each person lives his life, and which parallels the highest of all principles, that of free choice.

Man, by choosing wisely (between the two pillars,

most of which are hidden by the curtain), can raise himself up.

Waite compares this principle to the gift of the poet who can combine words to form a wondrous creation — we either have this ability or we don't have this ability, and the power of "have" is equal to the power of "have not." But the rule of justice does not involve alternatives!

The columns of justice open the gate to one world — while the columns of the high priestess open up into another world!

12 The Hanged Man

THE HANGED MAN.

The gallows from which the man is hanging is the form of a "Taoist" cross, while the figure forms the shape of the cross with his feet. Around the head of The Hanged Man is a halo in the form of a wreath.

It is important to understand that the "Taoist" cross is a cross of punishment — the Romans would punish people through crucifixion, and reverse crucifixion (head downwards), which also signifies humiliation. But The Hanged Man makes the cross with his feet, that is, he sacrifices himself, thereby achieving a degree of holiness.

Furthermore, the gallows is made from a tree which has the power of life — that is the meaning of the leaves!

The face of The Hanged Man does not express sadness, but a sense of "trance." The entire figure is the image of life, rather than the image of death.

The meaning of the card is not entirely clear, and it can be interpreted in different directions. There are those who even see this card as the tortured saint. But the proper approach is to see The Hanged Man as suspended between heaven and earth, between the divine and the material. The Hanged Man has given up the material (head facing down) but has not yet reached the divine — but he is on his way there!

There are those who see the card as hinting that there is renewed life after death — resurrection.

13 Death

DEATH.

This card, more than anything else, symbolizes change, a transition from a lower stage to a higher stage. Indeed, this card is controlled by a skeleton dressed in armor riding on a horse, a white horse, and only half of him is visible. In other words, the card does not reveal the whole picture. As opposed to the horse, the flag is black (with the rose in the center again white).

The images at the feet of the horse symbolize the cycle of life — childhood, adolescence, adulthood, old age. The cycle of life, the fact that the card indicates change rather than the end, appear also in the river flowing to the rear, and the sun rising between the towers in the background.

Behind the horseman, in the background, is a world that is entirely spiritual. The mysterious horseman, rides slowly and carries the symbol of the mysterious rose, the symbol of life. The rising sun is eternal.

The power of the card is in the power of the horseman — he does not carry any weapon, and yet a king (wearing a crown), a young maiden and a child stand before him in surrender.

In contrast with the previous card The Hanged Man, where the death is "mystical," the death here is substantial — the transition of man through the various stages of the cycle of life, inevitably brings him to the final stage — death. But while man is still alive, death, in his eyes, is mysterious, mystical, hiding behind the towers which lead to the kingdom of the unknown. Therefore, occultists interpret this card, whose number is 13 (a number which portends good or evil, according to human culture) as representing rebirth, creation, renewal, and not death in its literal sense.

14 Temperance

TEMPERANCE.

A winged angel with the symbol of his sun on his head, and on his chest is a triangle within a square, together with the letters of the Tetragrammaton, which indicates perfect balance. It is important to understand that the concept of "angel" here does not represent a man nor a woman — the figure has no defined sexuality. The angel is pouring the fluid of life from one cup to another. One of his bare feet is in the water while the other foot is on the ground — the essence of nature. There is a path which leads uninterrupted towards the high mountains, above which there is tremendous light shining in the shape of a radiant crown. This light shows us that man can attain merit and spiritual illumination, but the way there is long and difficult.

The symbols on the card indicate changes in the seasons, perpetual cyclical motion, and a combination of ideas, the blending of male and female. There are researchers who claim that this card symbolizes the third part of the Trinity within man (which is expressed in his ability to reach illumination). The symbol of the sun on his forehead can hint at "the third eye" through which man can see divine illumination. This card is called Temperance because when we attain the attribute of the card, various components of our human temperament combine to form a single harmony, which combines the psychic and the material. Thus we can understand with our logic, whence we are coming and where we are going.

(It is important to understand that the combination of the triangle within the square, together with the letters of God's Ineffable name, are the essence of the tarot — the triangle represents the 21 cards of the Major Arcana, the card of The Fool, the "0" card, represents the self and does not participate in this game, and on each side of the triangle there are seven cards. The square represents the 56 cards of the Minor Arcana, 14 cards on each side. The letters י-ה-ו-ה indicate a spiral ascent from stage to stage within the Major Arcana of the tarot cards).

15 The Devil

THE DEVIL .

The card of "The Devil" is an interesting card, primarily because of the combination, the harmony, between several motifs. We see the satyr, the goat with curved horns and bat's wings, standing on an altar. His hairy legs and claws like those of a bird of prey, together with the tail indicate his animalistic nature. The position of his legs, and the hair flowing between them, indicate sexual licentiousness (in contrast with the man and woman, his pupils, who are completely exposed!)

The stomach of the Devil bears the symbol of Mercury. His right hand is raised up, but the movement of his hand is the reverse of the priestly blessing we saw in card no. 5. In his left hand he holds a large torch, pointed downwards, towards the source of the Devil's fire, rather than towards the sun, the source of the blessed fire. On the devil's forehead there is a upside-down pentagram.

In the front of the altar is a ring, from which there are two chains bound to the necks of the man and the woman. Once again, we can see a similarity to the fifth card, but also to the third card — Adam and Eve who were bound to the Devil when they were banished from the Garden of Eden. The chains represent the chains of the material world and the fact that the hands of the images are free represents their ability to remove the chains from around their necks at any time.

The figures of the man and woman, the Devil's disciples, have horns and tails, similar to the Devil, but on their faces we can recognize human wisdom, that the Devil which stands above them will not necessarily be their master forever.

The background in which the Devil works is black, night. Furthermore, the torch is lowered. The upside-down pentagram indicates that the five senses do not work here. Only Divine Providence can rescue the chained figures from the hands of the Devil.

16 The Tower

THE TOWER.

The Tower, the "Tower of Babel" or the "Lightening-Struck Tower" generally symbolizes destruction in any area — this is the most obvious expression of this card. There are many who claim that The Tower actually symbolizes the folly of the material world — but this does not explain the inclusion of the columns and towers found on earlier cards. Others claim that this is the fall of man — the banishment from the Garden of Eden and therefore the card is black (falling from light into darkness).

But the more accepted approach sees this card as the process of materialization of the spiritual world. This is the fall of thought, the free spirit, which attempted to unlock the mysteries of the Creator. Perhaps we can say here: "With the help of God, even a broom can shoot" or "Only a tower founded in the will of God will be established in Heaven."

The falling figures, one who is wearing a crown, are frightened. The lightening hitting the tower (lightening is always a blow from God), a fire erupting, the darkness, the fact that in addition to all this, the tower is high and is also built on a mountaintop above a great abyss — all this doesn't leave the falling figures much hope. Notice that the "crown" of the tower is falling and the escape hatches — the windows — are in flames.

It is important to see that on the background of the darkness and the fire, there are "drops" of fire in the sky — ten of them on the side of the king who is wearing the crown, and twelve on the side of the other figure, a total of 22, which is the number of tarot cards in the entire Major Arcana, or the number of letters in the Hebrew alphabet, or the parts of the Tree of Life according to the Kabbala. This is the only chance for salvation — the ten spheres of the Tree of Life on the one side, or the twelve signs of the Zodiac on the other side.

Luckily, card no. 16 is followed by card no. 17, which can change our fate...

17 The Star

In the center of the card is a large eight-pointed star, surrounded by seven smaller stars, also with eight points. The female figure, completely naked, in the front of the card, has her left foot on the ground and her right foot in the water. She is pouring the water of life from two large jugs, one into the sea and one onto the land. Behind the female figure is a hill, on top of which is a tree, and on top of the tree is a bird.

The figure represents youth and beauty, but not necessary physical beauty. The nakedness reflects pure truth, innocence. The card is lit up, despite the fact that there is no sun, and that is the essence of the eight-pointed star, whose power is increased with the help of the number 7, of the smaller stars. This figure, which encompasses youth and virginal beauty, innocent, unites the elements while recognizing the lofty heavens. This is the reason that this card is sometimes referred to as "The Gifts of the Spirit" or "Well of the Waters of Life."

It is clear that this card indicates hope. This figure is the image of the naked truth, pure and lustrous in its beauty, giving the most precious thing in her hands — the waters of life. (Only a few of the interpreters see within this figure an expression of immorality and "the lower light.") In this sense she is the great mother of the sephira of "Binah" (understanding) from the Kabbala, with divine understanding, who showers her wisdom upon the lower spheres.

It is important to remember that the bird, which has the power to fly (its wings are spread as if ready to take flight) hints at man's ability to fly, to raise himself up towards the upper light, with the help of the pure truth.

18 The Moon

THE MOON.

The Moon is rising and we also see there a full moon, a crescent moon and a woman's face. The Moon has 32 beams — 16 short ones and 16 long ones. Beneath the moon we see two towers, and between them a dog and a wolf are howling at the moon, situated on either side of a path which leads into the hills. This path begins in a pool of water from which a crab is climbing out.

The card represents the life of the imagination — which is apart from the life of the spirit. The path which proceeds from the pool, between the towers into the hills represents the journey towards the unknown. The dog and the wolf represent the fears man has of the unfamiliar world, unlit, with only the moon to guide him on his way.

It is important to notice that the light in this card is merely reflected, an afterimage.

The analysis brings to another type of symbolism — the intellectual light is a reflection beyond which is the unknown mystery. This light reduces man's animal nature, represented by the dog, the wolf, and the crab emerging from the depths of the sea. This crab emerges and crawls out onto the land, but most of the time he falls back into the depths, symbolizing the difficulty in achieving the material.

It is important to distinguish the coldness, the iciness, with which the Moon looks down from above, raining down 15 drops of frost onto the strange scene below, as if she is spreading a frozen, forced peace onto the face of man. (There are those who interpret the 15 drops as being drawn to the moon, through the power of the tides it arouses, and therefore the Moon is moving the crab, the depths, the subconscious — to the land, the known — through its power of attraction.)

19 The Sun

THE SUN .

A naked child rides on a white horse, carrying a red banner, and behind him is a field of blossoming sunflowers. Above him shines a large sun, with a human face, and with alternating straight beams (visible) and wavy beams (hidden): 21 visible beams and one beam partly hidden. The strong light is an expression of the holy light, the divine, which lights the path of humanity. The source of the light is behind the garden wall (the Garden of Eden?). The 21 sun beams hint at the tarot cards, and the hidden light beam hints at the 22nd card — The Fool.

This card hints at the transition from the manifest light on the surface of the earth, the terrestrial, represented by the sun, to the hidden light of the world to come — a world represented by the innocent image of the naked child.

It is important to understand an additional level of the symbolism — the Sun is the consciousness of the sprit, direct and penetrating (in contrast with the reflected light, the afterimage of The Moon, card no. 18). The child, a simple and innocent figure, virginal, represents the seed of the spirit in which the essence of wisdom is found. This seed will save and preserve the world. The earthly light and the heavenly light are made to unite as the small child develops.

This is a very important card, which more than anything else, indicates the hope for a better future.

20 Judgment

The day of Judgment, which is also the day of the Resurrection or the day on which the dead are "judged," is a card that has hundreds of different versions in various tarot decks, but the different versions all maintain the identical principles.

A large angel flanked by clouds, blowing a trumpet which bears a banner with a cross. The dead are rising from their graves: a woman to the right, a man to the left and a child in the center, with their backs facing us. In the background there are more figures, an additional family. All the figures are raising their hands and faces in a movement which has an element of wonder and ecstasy, towards the angel.

It is important to understand that this card is the fulfillment of the prayer in our hearts — renewed life. This a most important moment where the inner prayers are fulfilled through divine power.

The trumpet, which leads the angel, is a symbol of the inner voice, which tries to reach up to God Almighty, and it pulls with it the rest of the human body. Understanding this process, recognizing the inner voice, is what enables us to believe in eternal life (in this sense, this card is similar to card no. 14, Temperance).

Notice that in contrast with the card of "The Lovers" where the Lovers have their backs to the king, in this card the faces of the figures are facing upwards, towards the angel, and it is as if they are "drawn" to the angel while on the card of "The Lovers," the woman and the man are facing towards the ground.

21 The World

THE WORLD.

This card, which sometimes appears following The Fool's card, is the last card in the Major Arcana, and this card actually closes the cycle through which we have passed, but on a higher level, with a deeper awareness. This card represents the perfection, the exquisite end of the cosmos — the elements within it and an expression of the World's understanding of the recognition of God.

This card also represents the soul, the consciousness — the divine vision which exposes the soul that knows itself. When the past is formulated alongside proper recognition, the world will be a better place, as the symbols of the card tell us. A world in which spiritual perfection reigns.

(There are interpretations which see this card as symbolizing the great magician, the wise sorcerer, who controls the inner and outer worlds through the knowledge he has acquired, which is symbolized by the pair of wands and the four symbols. Another interpretation, which is also common, is one which sees in this card control of woman's sexuality, femininity, the world — notice what the "flowers" in the wreath surrounding the figure resemble!)

In this card we see a feminine figure, naked, with a red scarf covering her in a spiral fashion. It is important to notice that her genitals are covered — this is no longer an "innocent" figure. Surrounding the figure is a wreath, tied together, symbolizing eternity, perpetual motion. In the hands of the figure are two wands, that is to say, all knowledge and power rests in the hands of the figure. Surrounding her there are four images, which represent the four elements, the four seasons — man, eagle, lion and ram; or, alternatively, human, a bird, animal of prey, beast. The combination of four — symbolizing the solid foundation, as well as the circle surrounding the figure, give us a sense of perfect balance.

0 The Fool

This card sometimes has the number 21 (and then The World is card no. 22), or 22. But its meaning does not change. We see a young man, stepping lightly alongside the abyss, above the mountains, as if no law controls him, and he has no fear in his heart. (This is the source of the name, "Fool," here he fools around all over the world and pays no attention to the dangers). He looks up at the sky in front of him, and it is important to note that even though he is situated high in the sky, his gaze is cast upwards. Notice that the sun is behind him, lighting the path in front of him! The young man has not yet decided where to turn — the dog jumps beside him as if asking him which way to go. In this card there is no sense of fear, or terror, despite the open abyss (and compare this, for example, with The Tower card). An angel is watching the young man's steps.

The image of the young man represents spiritual man, free from all material limitations. A figure whose face is intelligent, as if he sees a daydream before his open eyes. In one hand the young man holds a white rose, and this is a symbol of perfect purity. In his other hand he holds a staff on which hangs a purse that appears to be valuable. The young man is holding the staff and the purse with two fingers, which shows that the material — the purse — doesn't concern him. He is a prince from another world, making his way in the light of the morning sun, in the clear air. He is a soul in search of the human experience — we do not know which way he will turn, or if he will return from his journey, or when he will return. This card represents the symbolism of the human experience. In actuality, all directions are stretched out before him, and the laurel leaves and feather on his head hint that "wherever he turns — he will be successful."

When we discuss the interpretations of the cards and the different spreads for the purpose of fortune-telling and character analysis, we will see that "The Fool" card is a key card, perhaps the most important card the moment it is opened. This card can break, in essence, the existing framework and makes us search for new, complete and perfect frameworks.

INTERPRETING THE CARDS IN THE MAJOR ARCANA

Before we discuss interpreting the tarot cards of the Major Arcana (the first 22 cards), we should discuss a bit about the concept of interpretation itself, and present the factors affecting this process.

When we speak about "interpreting," we refer to the meaning we attribute to each card when we wish to analyze one's character, see the past (reincarnations), or foretell the future using the cards. We refer to a particular card the querent chooses, and give it the proper interpretation according to the position of the card within the spread.

With tarot cards, each card has a definite meaning, although within quite a broad range — its interpretation changes according to the position of the card in the spread, the cards which precede it or follow it in the spread, and of course, whether it is a "upright" card (direct card) or a "reverse" card (that is, whether the querent sees the card as facing him "upright," so that he can read what is written on it, or if he sees it in "reverse").

Some of the spreads, or the methods used to display the cards, refer only to the card, without considering whether it is "upright" of "reverse." But all of the spreads assign a great deal of importance to the order in which the cards are revealed, and to the relationship between each of the cards.

Actually, interpreting each card on its own is very simple — one can keep a list featuring all of the cards, like fortune-telling cards that come out of a machine. But deeper thought, and herein lies the real ability of the interpreter, is needed to combine the cards with each other, together with the order in which they appear. There is a vast difference between the tarot card reader who knows all the details of the tarot cards, and the inexperienced amateur.

We can divide the interpretation process into three components:

1. The ability of the tarot card reader.

The ability of the one who lays out the cards to see what is being asked, to understand its essence. This, in reality, is the ability of a "medium" who uses the cards as one of his tools.

Any reading of the cards requires a certain degree of "ability" as a medium, and this is the most obvious difference between various tarot card readers. The same cards, the same spread, the same order of cards — will result in two different interpretations from two different mediums. And this is all right. Just the way the same cake recipe will yield cakes that are different — either to a greater or lesser degree — from different bakers!

We cannot ignore this factor. Occasionally, amateurs tend to look for identical readings when interpreting the tarot cards. This is really quite impossible. The fact is that different mediums, even regarding the same querent and the same card set up will offer different interpretations.

2. The cards the reader uses.

There are several thousand sets of tarot cards. Despite the vast variety, there is a great deal of similarity among sets — the number of cards, the figures and images that appear on the cards, the numbering, etc. To a large extent similarities outnumber the differences.

We have selected one set of cards, the Rider-Waite deck of tarot cards, which is the most accepted and the deck to which most books refer. Each card in the two Arcanas has a name and a number (and the number is related to a certain Hebrew letter). In other decks we can find that each card has a name, a number and a Hebrew letter.

It is obvious that these three things are the basics of interpretation — a card whose name is "Day of Judgment" has a different interpretation from the one called "The Lovers," for example; the card numbered 1 has a different meaning than the card numbered 2.

Therefore, before any interpretation, the tarot card reader must suit the cards to the interpretation. There are decks of cards in which the "Strength" and "Justice" cards are switched, there are decks in which the location of "The Fool" card is different, or "The World" card. These changes sometimes create a difference in the numbering of cards — the numerological interpretation — and the letters on the cards — the Kaballistic interpretation.

Despite all the changes, the interpretations of the tarot cards are quite similar in all of the decks. The adaptations are fairly minimal.

3. Position of the card in the spread.

Since we already understand the significance of the medium and the importance of the interpretation of each and every card (as mentioned, taking into account the name of the card, the number and letter), we shall now analyze the position of the card within the spread.

The first thing is to ask whether the card is upright (direct) or reverse. In many methods of interpretation, we ignore this question completely, and each card has only one interpretation, which is either strengthened or weakened depending on its "environment" — the cards that are near that particular card. Other methods examine each card to see whether it is "upright" — that is, positive, or "reverse" — that is, negative.

Once we have selected the particular spread — we have also determined whether we will use upright/reverse or use a single interpretation for each card. Here we can determine the way in which the cards are combined with each other, and how the position of one card may affect another card.

Here, in the overall interpretation, is where the ability of the tarot card reader is expressed and a routine, mechanical interpretation becomes a work of art, many colored and multi-faceted, in which each person finds what he is looking for.

We will begin with the basics, that is, with the interpretation of each card. For each card we will give the basic interpretation, followed by an interpretation for the case of upright or reverse, positive or negative, so that you may use this information for all types of spreads, which will be discussed further later on.

(It is important to understand that a reverse card is, generally speaking, a negative direction of the attributes that can be seen when the card is upright. A gambler in a upright card will become a scoundrel in a reverse card, and so on. The principle is that the reverse card reinforces the negative attributes, while the upright card reinforces the positive attributes. This is true in almost all cases.)

[The Tarot cards in this chepter are from 2 decks from France].

1 The Magician

The Magician, the first card of the Major Arcana, bears the number "1," and the first letter of the Hebrew alphabet, א. From this it is clear that any interpretation of this card will have the numerological characteristics of the number 1, and the Kaballistic characteristics of the first letter. Therefore, the Magician is a male card, masculine, bursting with creative energy. It begins the cycle, or hints at the beginning of a new cycle (according to its location in the spread). Key words are masculinity, power, self-awareness, relationship between the heavenly and earthbound.

Upright: Skill, diplomacy, self-confidence, power of will, the means to "search heaven and earth," strong ego. But also, disasters, illness, and tremendous losses. This is a card which characterizes lawyers, medical professionals, gamblers, businessmen, and of course, magicians or those dealing in magic.

Reverse: Illusion, confusion, wizard, emotional problems, disgrace, unrest, unexpressed talent. Tendency towards fraudulent actions. Anticipated failure, perhaps even great failure.

2 The High Priestess

The High Priestess bears the second letter of the Hebrew alphabet, ב, and the number 2. It has the principle of woman, femininity. It is not the opposite of the first card, rather it complements it. The card hints at mystical power, and it is the type of card in which the hidden elements outnumber the obvious ones.

Upright: Secrets, mystery, hazy future, wisdom, knowledge, deep awareness that has not yet been revealed. Sometimes, this card indicates that the answers simply cannot be found.

Reverse: Desire, either physical or spiritual, dark secret, emotional instability. When the querent is a man — the card signifies problems with sexual identity. When the querent is a woman — the card signifies difficulties with the reproductive organs.

3 The Empress

The third letter of the Hebrew alphabet, ג, and the number 3. This is the queen of nature. She is Venus in the fullest meaning — feminine, contributing towards life and death, beginning the cycle of life.

Upright: Activity, motherhood, birth, success, sex, pregnancy, family, economic success, social activity. She determines the length of the day and exposes that which is hidden. But also distrust, doubt, mystery, and rudeness.

Reverse: Publicity, exposing secrets, possessiveness, jealousy, female problems, alienation from children, sexual depravity. But also revealing the truth (actually a positive aspect to a reverse card).

4 The Emperor

The Emperor, naturally, is a controlling card, a card with authority. A father figure, the first power on the earth. The number 4 and the fourth letter of the Hebrew alphabet, ד, symbolize this card.

Upright: Authority, stability, power, granting protection, a great person, help, strong will, courage, the top of the pyramid. A very important aspect is taking responsibility for the acts of others.

Reverse: Controlling, spreads confusion, exerts pressure, difficulties delegating authority, criticizing others. For a woman — difficulties with her husband, perhaps even violence. For a man — hides behind someone else's apron.

5 The Hierophant

The Hierophant, number 5 and the Hebrew letter ה represents the powers of morality, religion, values. His actions take place in the spiritual realm. This card also represents the family, which unites under the blessing of religion and morality.

Upright: Holy servitude, marriage, divorce, law, religious matters, conservatism, religious pleasures. Possibility of "captivity." Spiritual enlightenment, mercy, and compassion.

Reverse: Hypocrisy, greed, mourning, sexual offenses, great weakness. Over-politeness, to the point of obsequiousness. Destruction of the institution of family. Bad advice.

6 The Lovers

The card which bears the Hebrew letter **ו** and the number 6. This card represents sexual temptation, the choice between good and evil, between desire for the heavenly God, or striving toward the underworld. All issues relating to love of man, God, and heavenly morality.

Upright: Attraction, love, beauty, overcoming obstacles. Problems in love — choosing between different options at a crossroads. For a man — a challenge; for a woman — struggling.

Reverse: Difficulties in one's love life, failure, frustration in one's love life, fear, low sexual ability. In any case, a reversed "Lovers" card signifies problems with one's partner/spouse. For a man — possible impotency; for a woman — not maximizing her sexuality.

7 The Chariot

On this card appears the Hebrew letter ז and the number 7, and the fact that this is the last card of the first septet of cards is very significant. The first septet of the tarot cards deals primarily with matters of awareness and the spirit. The Chariot hints at the possibility of continuing to proceed forward, to the second septet (which deals primarily with the earthbound, physical aspects of a person's life).

Upright: Divine providence, possibility of advancing in life, victory, war (and winning it), fulfilled vengeance. Also, a possible indication of problems, ambition, overcoming fears, or hesitation.

Reverse: Quarrels, argument, defeat, accidents, difficulty moving from place to place, or from position to position. Also hints at the possibility of mental illness.

8 Strength

See the card in the Rider-Waite deck (p. 25), in which the woman subdues the king of beasts with her bare hands, represents physical strength, but also spiritual strength overcoming the physical. It bears the number 8, and the Hebrew letter ח.

(Often, this card is located in the 11th position, and the card of "Justice" appears here. In that case, this card bears the number 11, and corresponds to the Hebrew letter כ.)

Upright: Strength, energy, action, courage, fulfilling an objective, reaching the finish line. Controlling physical desire, good health, spiritual strength leading to spiritual expression (the power of healing or seeing the unknown).

Reverse: Tyranny, the power to corrupt, weakness, self-hatred, physical offenses, illness, perverse sexuality.

9 The Hermit

Card number 9, with the Hebrew letter ט. This is a clear illustration of an old man seeking his way, and searching for one's path is the main meaning of this card.

Upright: Enlightenment, wisdom, peace. But also apathy, corruption. This card enhances the other cards near it in the spread, and outlines the path.

Reverse: Mainly, alienation, fear, illogic. In other words, selecting the wrong path in life.

10 Wheel of Fortune

The Wheel of Fortune, the Wheel of Fate, the card that indicates change. More than anything, this card indicates the circle of life, change from one situation to another, as is normal. The Hebrew letter **י** and the number 10 (this card ends the first set of 10 cards, and is the first card to have two digits, very significant in terms of its numerology).

Upright: Fate, success, good luck. Change towards a positive direction. Winning a gamble. A pleasant surprise. A person in control of his life.

Reverse: No luck, instability, giving in to fate, lack of confidence. In certain spreads of cards apathy, stopping of the wheel (death).

11 Justice

In the Rider-Waite deck this card bears the number 11 and the Hebrew letter כ (p. 31). Here it has been switched with card number 8, "Strength". This card primarily indicates the realm that its name signifies (see p. 68).

Upright: Sincerity, honesty, the triumph of the law, recognition of social frameworks, reward, and punishment.

Reverse: Law, coercion, feelings of guilt, hypocrisy, double meaning, imbalance.

12 The Hanged Man

The number 12, the Hebrew letter ל. The main interpretation is subordination of the physical in favor of the spiritual, the victory of the spirit over matter.

Upright: Wisdom, intuition, ability to prophesy, self-sacrifice, giving up the moment in favor of tomorrow, being an example to others.

Reverse: Selfishness, tendency to follow the crowd, political hypocrisy, punishment for sin, masochism, humiliating others.

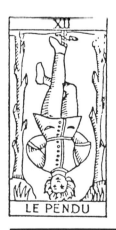

13 Death

Number 13 (which is most significant) and the Hebrew letter מ. The main interpretation of this card is the completion of one cycle and the beginning of another cycle (death — birth).

Upright: End, destruction, corruption, failure in marriage, loss of a spouse, loss of a position of strength.

Reverse: Loss of all hope, difficulties, death.

(This card is considered by most to be a bad card, in any position. When the card is upright, it is only "a little bit" bad. A reversed card increases the danger and brings it closer.)

14 Temperance

Number 14 (which completes another septet) and the Hebrew letter **ﬡ**. This card primarily indicates the path towards integration and cooperation with others, in order to advance both the individual and the community.

Upright: Moderation, patience, economic success, management ability. Compromise, talent for science, talent for the arts.

Reverse: All things related to blind religious faith. No luck, problems, mood swings, antagonism, sometimes split personality, being two-faced, hypocritical.

15 The Devil

The Devil, card number 15 and the Hebrew letter ס, is usually interpreted as the subject of the card. This card symbolizes transition to a deeper spiritual dimension. This is the first card which depicts the struggle between darkness and light.

Upright: Energy, violence, expressed sexuality, lust, pride, physical weakness, addiction to pleasure, family problems, work-related problems, exaggerated charisma (destructive), leadership.

Reverse: Evil influence, weakness, spiritual blindness, sexual corruption, addiction, tendency toward a life of crime. Whatever may be bad when this card is upright, becomes truly terrible when the card is reversed.

16 The Tower

Card number 16, with the Hebrew letter **ע**. This card primarily symbolizes the vanity of the material world, the shaky foundation of property for its own sake, without any spiritual power.

Upright: Suffering, destruction, degradation, depression. Collapsing relationships, shaky economic status. Accidents, illness, destruction of frameworks.

Reverse: A warning about all the evils of the upright card! A feeling that danger is threatening. (Notice that with this card, it is the reverse card that is better than the upright card.)

17 The Star

A symbol of hope, the possibility of a change for the better. It is important that this card be opened in any spread! This card always leaves room for the chance of a better future. Its number is 17, with the Hebrew letter ﬤ.

Upright: Hope for better circumstances, developing new talents, overcoming difficulties. But also setbacks, dangers, and illness.

Reverse: Illness, risk of death, disappointment, difficulties, impotence, hints that a person needs help from any direction.

18 The Moon

Card number 18 and the Hebrew letter **צ**. This card is a feminine card, and symbolizes feminine wisdom, which is accumulated, mysterious; sends a person to seek the advice of the wise spirit.

Upright: Warns against hidden enemies, warns of danger, mistakes the person has made, tendency towards mysticism. Overcoming difficulties.

Reverse: Instability, serious illness, the person needs help. This card is a very bad sign.

19 The Sun

The card of The Sun is number 19, and its Hebrew letter is **ק**. The main idea behind this card is the transition from darkness into great light.

Upright: Happiness, material satisfaction, successful marriage, love pouring into the person, self-confidence, respect.

Reverse: Difficulties, economic problems, a significant reduction of the meanings of an "upright" card, a difficult period in the person's life, dependency.

20 Judgment

Card number 20 (closing the second set of 10 cards), with the Hebrew letter ר. It indicates the handing down of justice, together with rebirth, or a new incarnation.

Upright: Change of status, rebirth, outcome, renewed sexuality, reward for the past, a new, successful beginning. Breaking off a bad relationship. A new door — leading to a second chance!

Reverse: Weakness, finality, austerity which leads to a lower status, loss, death, a beginning without end, lack of purpose, illness.

21 The World

Card number 21 (3x7, which is very important in numerology!) and the letter ת (the final letter). This is, in actually, the closing card.

Upright: Guaranteed success, change of location, immigration, good fortune, good sexual relationship, new acquaintance.

Reverse: Feeling of alienation, inability to complete things, failures, delays, desperation, obstacles.

0 The Fool

The card whose number is zero (0) (but which may also appear as number 1, 21, or 22 in different tarot decks). The Hebrew letter of this card is usually ש (but sometimes א or ת). This card primarily describes the shattering of frameworks, or the breaking of a spread. There are those who reshuffle the cards and lay out a new spread if this card appears.

Upright: Anything is possible, but not necessarily for the better; apathy, boredom, lack of caring, tendency towards addiction, madness... but with reasonable limits, new beginnings without any knowledge or "baggage" from the past.

Reverse: All the negative attributes of the upright card, but much more serious. Stagnation, total apathy.

LE MAT

22 LE FOU

BEFORE REVEALING THE CARDS

When we are familiar with the meanings of the cards in the deck we have chosen, when we understand the significance of the cards and their relationship with each other, there is one more step to go over before discussing the various card spreads that determine the relationship between the cards and the meaning the reader interprets for the querent.

This step holds true for any series of cards we elect to use — the 22 cards of the Major Arcana, the 56 cards in the Minor Arcana, or the 78 cards in a full tarot deck, which includes both the Major and Minor Arcanas.

We can call this step, **"atmosphere."**

When we open the cards, we receive messages through them — vibrations, which the querent transmits to us, through which we receive answers to questions from that source, or from another source.

It is obvious, for example, that if the person sitting across from us is nervous and impatient, we can immediately see that the messages he is broadcasting are those of worry and stress.

In order to receive those messages, we must prepare the proper atmosphere, and this is done on four levels: the querent, the tarot reader, the location, and the cards one uses.

When the querent approaches the tarot reader, the reader must evaluate his situation. There is no point in opening the cards for someone who is in a critical state — whether overly nervous, or overly at ease to the point of overt ridicule, as it just will not work!

When a person knowingly declares that he does not believe in the cards, this is not necessarily a limitation — but when someone is constantly looking at his watch and stating he has no time... cancel the reading and schedule another session.

It is important that the tarot card reader "knows with whom he is dealing." If the querent who is looking at his watch is someone familiar, it is possible to explain to him that the atmosphere just is not right. If you do not know the querent, just gently reschedule the reading for another time.

The same is true for the tarot reader himself — when he feels that he is not "at his best" — for example, if something is troubling him, or he is tired and cannot concentrate — it is best to postpone the reading for another time.

Regarding the surroundings, it is important that the opening of the cards, the spread, be done in a quiet location, preferably when the querent and the reader are alone. A tarot card reader who takes his profession seriously can give a querent a quick reading in a public place or on a stage, but a deeper reading should always be saved for a quiet and subdued place, where the reader and querent can be alone.

The cards the reader uses should be in good condition, and treated with respect. It is customary to keep them covered with a cloth, and it is best to keep them in a container made of paper, wood, or leather — never plastic or metal! The cards must be kept clean and whole.

When one touches the cards, it should be done with clean hands. There are those who wash their hands right before a reading. The table should be covered with a cloth, with no extraneous objects on it (although there some readers who might keep a crystal or precious gem on the table, in order to keep any negative energy from damaging the atmosphere).

The tarot card reader is the one who touches and shuffles the cards — no one else ever touches his cards! Shuffling the cards should take about two minutes. During this time the reader should concentrate on the querent sitting opposite him — the querent should always sit opposite the reader — and try to receive his messages (even before the cards are actually opened).

No matter what type of opening, the type of cards, or the spread being used, one must always move from the light to the heavy. In other words, begin with simple questions and continue to the more difficult and significant questions. Never deal with "annoying" or "petty" questions. Remember that the cards only point the way — but the querent is the one who must decide if he will walk that path!

The more information you have about the querent, your answers will be more precise. But, on the other hand, such information can be an energetic obstacle to the messages the querent is broadcasting. You must find the middle road, the "golden path," between the information and the message, between the revealed and the hidden. This balance can only be achieved after a great deal of time and experience.

When you have serious news — illness, death, departure, loss, etc. — look at the cards again and consider very carefully how to give the querent his difficult response, or message. Never argue with the querent. The reader states what he sees in the cards. Period. The querent is free to either accept or reject the answer to his question.

And now, once the appropriate atmosphere has been set, we can begin to understand the types of spreads and card combinations.

THE SPREADS

Query Spread

When using the 22 cards of the Major Arcana, it is often customary to use a spread which is known as the Query Spread. To a certain extent this is a "personal" spread, as it has no specific rules, with the exception of shuffling the cards and cutting the deck. After that has been done, the reader attempts to answer a question posed by the person sitting across from him.

Let us say that a woman has come to the tarot card reader, and asks to know if she can expect to find a husband in the near future. The reader briefly states the question, any way he sees fit: "Will I marry?" "When will I marry?" "Will I find a husband soon?"

Why do we stress this process? Because this is a personal process, in which the reader directs the cards towards the question. After he has stated the question, he opens up a single card for each word in the question. No more and no less. This is very important, and this must be taken into account when the reader attempts to state the question.

The question "When..." is different from the question "Will I..." and therefore, even if the same card is revealed, its interpretation will be different for the two questions. The Moon card (18), indicates "in a short time" regarding the question "When," but communicates "Who can tell, it is still in the process of taking place" to the question "Will I."

After the question has been phrased and the cards laid out, we interpret each word according to the card that has been laid out adjacent to it. There are those who attach more importance to the final card that has been opened, and there are those who open an additional card (a helping card) to summarize the answer.

In the Query Spread, we use no more than five cards. It is not customary to answer more than three questions at a time, and it is important to shuffle and cut the cards following each question.

The Query Spread is an effective spread for the experienced tarot card reader, who controls the secrets of the tarot cards, knows how to phrase the question appropriately, and is familiar with the hidden relationships between the cards.

In the Query Spread, it is customary to use the interpretation based on whether the card is upright or reverse.

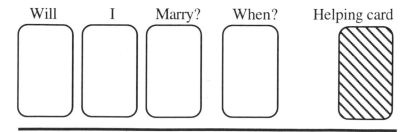

| Will | I | Marry? | When? | Helping card |

Palm of the Hand Spread

The Palm of the Hand Spread is a five-card spread. It bears the name Palm of the Hand because when the cards in this spread are laid out, they should correspond to each finger of the hand — from the thumb on the right side, through all of the fingers — and the astrological properties associated with each finger. Even though we call this the Palm of the Hand spread, we will relate to it as to a regular card spread, without considering its astrological aspect.

The Palm of the Hand spread is, in actuality, a repeat of the three-card spread (p. 93) — past, present, future — in which we open three cards that relate to the past (on the querent's right), the present (center) and the future (the querent's left). But the Palm of the Hand spread expands on this somewhat. We shuffle the cards, cut the deck, and lay out five cards, from left to right. The middle card is the present, and because it also hints at the subject about which the querent is asking (love, money, health, etc.) it holds more importance.

The first card to the left hints at the distant past, in which the querent was, in essence, dependent upon others (parents). The second card hints at the more recent past, in which he stood on his own two feet. The middle card is, as we said, the present. The fourth card hints at the immediate future, and the fifth card indicates the distant future, in which the person will, once again, be dependent upon others.

The interpretation is done, in this case, from the middle outward. In other words, we begin with the middle card, through which we determine the opening subject to be discussed on the basis of that middle card — spiritual or material, hope or depression, love or pain, etc. Once we have determined the subject, we analyze the row of cards, along a time line that passes through the person's life cycle.

With this spread, we do not usually use the upright/reverse method.

Under no circumstances should you open another card once the five cards have been laid out. This is a good method to use in order to understand the querent's nature and background, and his principle problems, his essence.

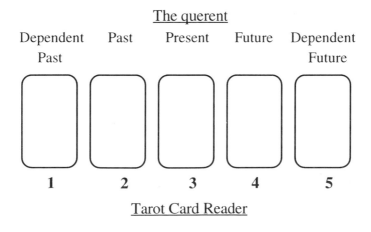

The querent

Dependent Past	Past	Present	Future	Dependent Future
1	2	3	4	5

Tarot Card Reader

Table Spreads

Table spreads are the simplest types of spreads, and their purpose is to provide a quick response to a particular subject. These are spreads that can also be done in a public place, or from a stage. Despite the simplicity of the spread, they contain a great deal of magic — precisely for the reason that they use a minimum number of tarot cards and concentrate on one subject, which forces the reader to utilize his maximum power.

A table spread can be done with a full deck, but the most common way to do it is to use the 22 tarot cards in the Major Arcana.

Prepare the cards, shuffle them, and cut the deck into two. The querent points to one of the piles (or the reader chooses the pile if he is doing the reading for himself). From here on in, the cards remain in the hands of the tarot card reader.

From the pile chosen, the reader opens the cards in order. Table spreads can consist of either one card, three cards, or four cards. Prior to laying out the cards, it is important to determine whether the reader will be using the upright/reverse method, or a single interpretation.

(In the examples that follow, we will relate to the single interpretation, without considering the question of whether the card is reverse or upright.)

1. Single Card Method

The tarot reader opens one card — the top card of the chosen pile. If it is The Fool card, another card is taken, and only that one is considered. The question should be one to which we can give a **yes** or **no** answer, or some other definitive answer, such as choosing between two clear options.

We open the card, and answer the question. If the querent has an additional question, we can place an additional card on top of the first card, and then we refer only to the second card. Under no circumstances should we link the cards when we use the single card method! Each card is designated for one question — and one answer.

Do not answer more than three questions for a single querent.

Will I be successful at work this month?

...No!

Will I marry soon?

...Yes!

Am I in any danger?

...No!

2. Three Card Method

Take the deck of cards after the cards have been shuffled and cut the deck into two piles. The querent chooses a pile. The reader lays out three cards, from left to right, and places the remaining cards to his right.

The cards in this order, represent the past (the card on the reader's left), the present (the middle card) and the future (the card on the reader's right), as shown in the illustration below.

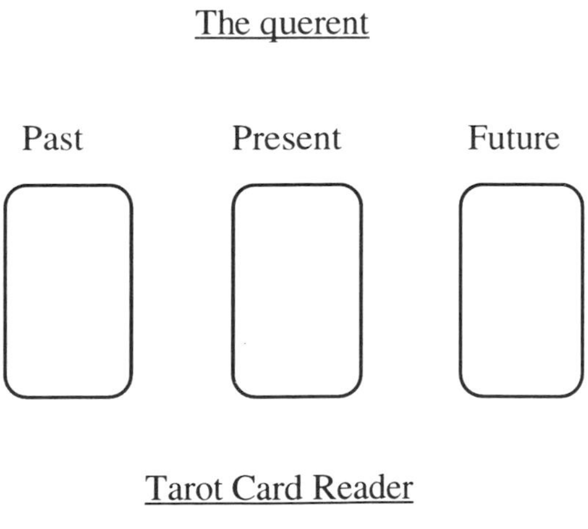

The querent

Past	Present	Future

Tarot Card Reader

This spread is the most common of the table spreads.

We can use this spread to analyze the querent's background, what stage he is at, what sort of "baggage" he is carrying with him, and what the future holds for him. The answers here are not yes/no answers. In essence, the querent is not asking a question, rather he waits for what the tarot reader has to say. (If the querent has a specific question, at the end of the spread the reader can proceed to a four-card spread, using either the current spread before him, or laying out a new spread.)

In this spread, the reader's ability to bring all his accumulated knowledge into play is really put to the test. He must decide, during a fraction of a second, what will be the guiding card, what are the most significant card combinations in the spread before him, and what is the overall picture he will give to the querent.

The tarot reader who is not expert in the meanings of the cards and isn't "sharp" enough to make the right combinations will discover that this spread, although apparently simple, can be full of obstacles. Conversely, the reader who is skilled in his craft will discover that this is the best of the basic spreads.

3. Four Card Method

This spread, is similar to the previous spread. But here we add a fourth card, which gives us a final answer, a summary, of the three first cards to be laid out.

Shuffle and cut the cards as you did previously. Open three cards and lay them out as with the previous spread.

The fourth card is placed on the side, either face up or face down (and then it is revealed only after the first three cards have been laid out).

Now, we interpret the three cards using the past/present/future system.

Then we ask the question, "What happens now?" and we must provide a definitive answer, such as yes or no, or another definite form.

Now we turn to the fourth card, using it to summarize the entire picture (taking into account the first three cards) and provide a definite answer.

Past   Present   Future

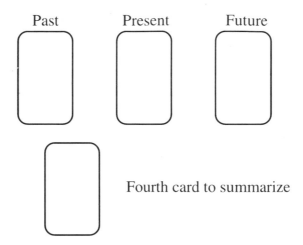

Fourth card to summarize

Examples

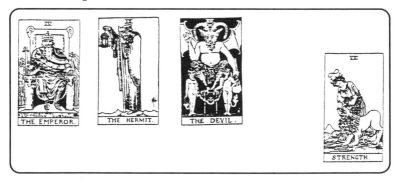

In this spread, the middle card is the signifier, or leading card, which indicates looking for one's way. In light of this card, the other cards should be interpreted and the proper conclusion reached.

This is a unique spread, in which all the cards have images of powerful women. The reader must take these characteristics into account when interpreting the spread.

This is a spread in which the past and the future contradict each other, with no present card to balance out the picture. Unfortunately, the fourth card presents us with a difficult picture, without providing a possibility for solution.

Seven Card Spread

The seven card spread is the last spread that can be done with the 22 cards of the Major Arcana. Seven cards to be revealed out of a total of 22 is a large number, and it should be taken into account that an additional 3 cards are added in order to clarify the future.

This spread is also called the Image Spread, or the Pentagram Spread, (a five-pointed star), because a diagram of the spread creates the shape of a five-pointed star. Since the pentagram has a "heart," there are those who call this the Heart of the Star spread.

This spread is excellent for a general analysis of the person, primarily in the area of the present. In actuality, the spread summarizes everything that has happened up to now in various aspects of the subject's life — character, family, work, education, thoughts, despairs, hopes. The future, indeed, is somewhat shortchanged in this spread, and therefore three cards can be added after we have finished reading the cards. These three extra cards will give us, in a separate reading, the direction towards which the person will turn.

It is important to understand that each card has its own area, defined and unique. Therefore, we must lay the cards out in the correct order, one after the other, and interpret them in their proper order. This spread makes substantial use of the upright/reverse system.

Shuffle the cards, cut the deck, and choose seven cards, in order, using the same methods we learned in the previous spreads. The diagram shows you the proper sequence for laying out the cards, and you must make sure to form the shape of the five-pointed star. Pay particular attention to cards 1 and 2. Card 2 covers card 1 horizontally. This is the only card in the spread that **may not** be interpreted using upright/reverse!

This spread can also be used with the Minor Arcana, 56 cards, and especially when we are using a full deck of tarot cards (78 cards). It is also useful with regular playing cards and in a spread using palm cards, which link the tarot reading with palm reading!

In order to study the meanings of the spread, we recommend practicing by jotting down notes on the results — using a table containing seven columns.

On the table write down the seven cards that were laid out, upright or reverse, and then try to form a question concerning each card. For example, for the fourth card — did the subject come from a loving family? For the second card — has the person fulfilled his desires? And the like.

In any case, remember that the overall picture of the querent is learned here, in the spread of the cards, through the details. But we must not conclude from this that each of the seven "cells" should provide a clear answer through the cards. Often you will discover that for a particular area, the card does not provide a clear answer. No matter. Go on, and remember that a person, just like the tarot, has more things hidden than things revealed.

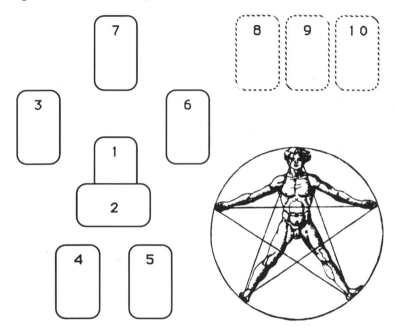

Each card has its own area:

1. From this card we learn about the querent's character.

2. From this card we learn about the person's fears, distress, and hopes.

These two cards are known as "the heart of the star." They deal with the spirit, and the burdens of the spirit.

Now we proceed to the left side, (and we continue around the spread in a clockwise direction).

3. This card teaches us about the area of the subject's work, his profession, and career.

4. This card teaches us about his family — origin and beginning — his status and birthplace.

5. This card teaches us about the position of the person in relation to his environment, his status at work and within the family, and what he has "achieved" in his lifetime.

6. This card tells us the direction of the person's current progress — is he ascending or descending, moving forward or backward, primarily in the material realm.

7. This card, the card at the "head," teaches us about the way the person thinks, his energy, his plans, the future, etc. This card is the most important, since it also teaches us what the person will do with the talents that have been cultivated within him up to this point.

(And in order to expand on this card, we can open the three additional cards that are placed beside the 7 card [from left to right]. These cards refer only to the subject's future, and card 7 serves as a jumping off point from which additional interpretations are made.)

THE MINOR ARCANA

There are 56 cards in the Minor Arcana, or the Lesser Arcana, of the tarot deck, which are divided, as we know, into suits: There are four suits – Cups, Wands (Clubs), Pentacles (Coins or Discs) and Swords. Each suit has 10 cards in a series, numbered from one (Ace) to ten, and these also have a numerological meaning that we will discuss later on. Each suit has three additional cards, the Court Cards – King, Queen and Knave (Page).

As mentioned, we have 40 numbered cards, and 12 court cards that correspond to the 12 signs of the Zodiac (giving them an additional astrological meaning). Furthermore, there are four Knight cards, whose principle meaning is "a new path" or "an ability that isn't utilized," and they point at new vistas that open up onto the picture.

We will briefly survey the meaning of each suit, and then look at the meaning of the 56 individual cards and their interpretations. Some of the cards possess a double meaning – both positive and negative (upright/reverse, or according to their position in the spread, as we shall discuss later on). Others of the cards are always interpreted in only one way, either positive or negative.

Since this book is intended for beginners, albeit at a high level, we will try to understand the basic meaning behind each card in the Minor Arcana.

THE SUITS

Cups

This suit is associated with the element Water in nature and, therefore, the world of emotion, the connection between a couple, intuitive ability and the ability to share with your partner. These cards are most important in questions relating to happiness and love, and realizing one's expectations from life.

This suit is comparable with the hearts suit in a regular deck of playing cards.

Wands

Associated with the element Fire, and therefore, a person's talents and skills. It is most important in identifying internal obstacles and challenges and pressures from the past, and to understand the individual's internal balance and his status vis-à-vis his environment.

This suit is comparable with the clubs suit in a regular deck of playing cards.

Pentacles

This suit is associated with the element Earth, and is therefore related to practical matters, such as wealth, the power to make things happen, creativity, health, willpower, etc. With this suit, it is important to see the card's position within the spread, since it has many ups and downs.

This suit is comparable to the diamonds suit in a regular deck of playing cards.

Swords

This suit is associated with the element Air, and also deals apparently, with logic, honest intelligence and one's ability to "make decisions." It is a difficult suit, with multiple interpretations, since for each card you must consider the positions of the other cards in the spread. To a certain extent, this suit shows us the "destiny" of the person himself.

This suit is comparable with the spades suit in a regular deck of playing cards.

Knight cards

The four Knights represent, as mentioned above, the "jokers" of life, which afford us with new opportunities. We will discuss these separately.

Cups

Ace (1) of Cups

The Ace of Cups is always a positive card. The illustration depicts a hand issuing from a cloud, bearing a Holy Grail from which the five senses are descending into the large subconscious reservoir of man and the Universe. The water lilies below determine the card's positive direction, and the dove situated above the cup also has a positive meaning.

Happiness, love, romance, strong emotions, fertility.

Two of Cups

The Two of Cups is a positive card, in the area of relationships.

Notice the symbolism of the card – the twisted snakes of the caduceus, the lion's head with the eagle's wings – all these symbolize elevation, shared radiance. The crowns hint at a positive direction, as well as the hands that reach out to each other in "togetherness."

Connection, love, family, harmony, strong emotion, compromise.

Three of Cups

The Three of Cups brings us the lovely maidens, adorned with flowers and wearing colorful robes, symbolizing a celebration or other happy occasion. The raised cups signify wine.

Positive – freedom, happiness, love, wholeness, positive sexuality.

Negative – pleasure-seeking, multi-faceted sexuality, instability

Four of Cups

The Four of Cups is a card whose interpretation is determined on the basis of its position within the spread. We see a completely apathetic man sitting beneath a tree, (which isn't a fruit tree), and he is waiting for something, but we don't know what.

Is this the peace of a person who has fulfilled himself, or the passivity of a person who is bored, lacking energy, lazy? The card's position in the spread will supply us with the answer.

Five of Cups

The Five of Cups is a card that is clearly negative. The figure represents bereavement, despair, and this, it is important to emphasize, is found in the number 5, which symbolizes the Pentagram, the person. There are overturned cups, and deserted buildings in the background.

This card also reflects negatively on the cards that are near it in the spread.

Six of Cups

The Six of Cups is a card that has many connections and interpretations. The cups and flowers indicate a positive direction, but the fact that the flowers are found inside the cups is indicative of an opportunity that has been missed.

This card is rich with symbolism – the headdress is that of a royal subject (rather than of a ruler). The knight's shield, houses, the soldier in the background, and so on.

Positive – a past that is pleasant to remember, which had a positive outcome.

Negative – the person did not turn his past into success for the present.

Seven of Cups

The Seven of Cups is a negative card, primarily because the black image is seen with its back towards us. The images on the card symbolize imagination, mysticism, and each cup bears the "promise" of something else.

But the position of the figure indicates that this is all imagined, or merely wishful thinking, and the person does not realize the possibilities. There are those who call this card the "Seven of Illusions" (of "Fantasies").

Eight of Cups

The Eight of Cups is a negative card. The person in the red robe is "yielding" to his despair, and is turning towards the barren mountains. He has left eight cups standing behind him, which symbolize his life's work. The moon looks at him questioningly.

This is a card of desperation, and can only be reversed if it is followed by a positive card.

Nine of Cups

The Nine of Cups is a positive card. We can describe the figure as a man sitting "beneath his cups," and all his desires have been fulfilled.

Notice the curtain behind the man, indicating that the future is shrouded in mystery.

Ten of Cups

The Ten of Cups is a card symbolizing perfect contentment. We see a family upon whom good fortune has smiled. This card, particularly when it comes to summarize a spread, can change the entire picture and promise a happy ending.

This card is most positive.

King of Cups

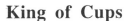

The King of Cups represents the zodiac symbol of Cancer. From an astrological point of view, this card represents the emotional baggage a person retains from his home and family.

When the card is **positive** it promises a stable and loving family. When the card is **negative** it hints at instability.

It has great influence, particularly on those whose astrological signs are Cancer or Pisces.

KING of CUPS.

Queen of Cups

The Queen of cups represents the astrological symbol of Scorpio. This card represents the subconscious, mysticism, the mysterious.

When the card is **positive** it can have many magical powers.

When the card is **negative** it mainly indicates evil.

This card is particularly influential on those whose astrological sign is Scorpio and Aquarius. It is an important card for understanding a person subconscious mind.

Page of Cups

The Page of Cups represents the astrological symbol of Pisces. This card represents the imagination.

When the card is **positive** it means the person has a well-developed imagination, with an emotional or creative bent.

When the card is **negative** the person is flighty, and may even be addicted to dreams and fantasies.

The card is particularly influential for those whose astrological sign is Pisces, Aquarius or Capricorn. It has a negative influence, primarily on people who have passed the age of adolescence.

PAGE of CUPS.

Wands

Ace (1) of Wands

The Ace of Wands is a positive card in any spread. A shining hand is peering out of a grey cloud, and in the background is a pastoral scene. In other words, if the person uses his skills, he can succeed in a creative, enterprising area, and advance in his life. The grasping of the wand, with the thumb parallel to the wand, shows that "everything rests in the hands of the person!"

Two of Wands

The Two of Wands is a card of "secrets revealed." The man is standing between two staves that form a gate; he looks out onto the horizon where there is a bay, but in his hand rests a globe of the entire world. We do not know what is to be – but the person may choose his own way!

Positive – initiative, planning, change.

Negative – the person looks far afield but doesn't see what is going on around him. He lives in a world of make-believe.

Three of Wands

The Three of Wands is the card for starting out on a journey. The person has his back turned to us, is dressed in a red robe and carries a staff with him (the two other staves remain behind as a "gate" to the rear of him).

Notice that nothing can really be seen in the horizon, but there is also nothing behind the person or at his feet. The interpretation of this card depends on the other cards that are near it. It can signify the opening of a new page... or can indicate that the person is running away from his responsibilities.

Four of Wands

The Four of Wands is a very positive card. The "canopy" adorned with garlands of flowers, the couple with their arms raised in gratitude, the solid structure behind them – all this signifies that the person knows how to combine the material and the spiritual, labor together with creativity. The positive influence of this card is reflected over the entire spread.

Incidentally, this is a card of twos, both in its number and its illustrations, and directs us towards relationships as the path to success.

Five of Wands

The Five of Wands appears to be a strange card: young men wearing strange clothes are battling, but as in a game.

Since the number five symbolizes the person, we interpret this card as signifying internal conflicts, a lack of direction. The question is whether the person will become stronger because of his internal struggles, or will he fall... this is the question posed by the entire spread.

The key idea here is struggle, or the internal battle.

Six of Wands

The Six of Wands is a positive card. It depicts a man's triumphant journey upon a white horse, and his head is decorated with a laurel wreath.

What could be better than this!

Notice that the man is accompanied by a crowd of people, in other words, he is a beneficent leader. This card indicates leadership and great success.

Seven of Wands

The Seven of Wands is a card of challenge. The person is standing on a hill, a staff in his hand, and although the staves of his enemies are lower than himself, they can still reach him!

Will the person be able to stand in the face of his enemies, or will he fail in this never-ending battle? Since the card can refer to an enemy or an internal struggle, the interpretation is obvious. A **positive** card indicates that the person will overcome all the obstacles in his way. A **negative** card indicates that the person will encounter conflicts and strife in all aspects of his life.

Eight of Wands

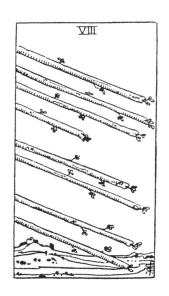

The Eight of Wands is a "graphic" card. It has no figures, but there is a hint of "greatness" upon the horizon (the castle). Notice that the division of the wands is 4-2-2.

The interpretation given to this card is based on the other cards in the spread. In principle, the card signifies flowing – things will occur, but their direction is unknown to us.

Nine of Wands

The Nine of Wands is a slightly unusual card. The person, despite the fact that he is surrounded by staves, is doing nothing. He rests upon a staff, and waits. There are those who see this card as a period of apathy, of stagnation, and therefore, as a negative card.

But there are those who interpret the card as a period of transition – the person is testing his way. It is clear that the card that follows this one in the spread will also determine the interpretation of the Nine of Wands.

Ten of Wands

The Ten of Wands is a negative card. The person is oppressed by the weight of the ten staves, despite the fact that they are arranged in a seemingly stable sheaf.

This card indicates that the person is overextended, trying to do more than he is capable of doing, and he is about to lose everything.

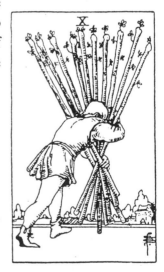

King of Wands

The King of Wands represents the astrological symbol for Aries. The card shows a King sitting upon a throne, and surrounding him are symbols of leadership and royalty – lions and salamanders.

When the card is **positive** the person has strength and initiative, creativity and daring. When the card is **negative**, the person is stubborn and violent, and if he holds a position of power – he is a menace to society.

This card is influential primarily on those whose astrological sign is Aries or Gemini.

Queen of Wands

The Queen of Wands corresponds to the astrological symbol of Leo. This card shows the ability to control, authority and leadership, which stem from the card's many symbols – the sunflower, the black cat, lions, etc.

But when the card is **negative**, then the person is arrogant and therefore, cannot be trusted.

The card is primarily influential for those whose astrological sign is Leo or Taurus

Page of Wands

The Page of Wands corresponds to the astrological symbol of Sagittarius. Notice the three pyramids appearing on the horizon.

When the card is **positive** the person seeks to expand his horizons, to utilize his skills and talents.

When the card is **negative**, the person is fearful of the mysterious future and holds himself back, to the point of idleness.

This card is primarily influential for those whose astrological sign is Sagittarius and Libra.

Pentacles

Ace (1) of Pentacles

The Ace of Pentacles is a positive card. A hand can be seen issuing from a cloud, holding a large pentacle. In the background is a flourishing garden, whose gate is open. The card indicates opportunities, possibilities, new plans. This is a positive card in the material world.

Two of Pentacles

The Two of Pentacles is a negative card, despite the fact that the figure depicted in the card is holding the symbol that represents "infinity." The unbalanced position of the symbol, together with the image of the clown and his movement (notice his feet) indicate that the card signifies instability in the person's material world.

To a large extent, fate plays a hand here, and does not allow the person the freedom to choose his destiny.

Three of Pentacles

The Three of Pentacles is a positive card. A man is seen standing, and he is higher than those who are listening to him. His audience appears to be prominent people, (while the man himself appears to be young). This indicates success in the area of one's career.

Notice that the three pentacles on this card appear in a solid column, above which is a building – once again, a symbol of material success!

Four of Pentacles

The Four of Pentacles is the card of someone "guarding his fortune." The other cards surrounding this card determine its interpretation.

The person is guarding his money, and could become a sullen miser. But he could also begin in a new field of endeavor with the help of the economic security with which his fortune endows him.

Five of Pentacles

The Five of Pentacles is a negative card, a severe one. The person depicted in the card has met with deprivation and poverty, while the wealth of others is visible through the window that is protected by bars. This is one of the worst cards in terms of the material world, and as a result, also the spiritual world. It affects the entire spread in a negative manner.

Six of Pentacles

The interpretation of the Six of Pentacles depends on the other cards in the spread. The person must make a decision – legal or administrative, or perhaps in the area concerning inheritance – that is likely to change his economic situation.

The question of whether the person is the giver or the receiver, the one with the wealth or the one asking to receive the wealth, is an open question. Notice that the scales in the picture are in perfect balance. This is a difficult card to interpret.

Seven of Pentacles

The Seven of Pentacles is a positive card. The card depicts an unfortunate person – his bearing is that of a laborer – looking at the wealth he has accumulated, which is growing and bearing fruit.

We do not know if the person is satisfied from his labors, but we do know that his labors have brought him material reward!

Eight of Pentacles

The Eight of Pentacles shows us a man who is building himself up, as well as his wealth, step by step. He is practical, thrifty, diligent, all of which bring him a "ladder" of coins, whose top reaches the heavens.

This is an important card for planning one's career.

Nine of Pentacles

The Nine of Pentacles indicates material success, which rests securely in the person's hand. Solid economic backing.

The fact that the image on the card is feminine reinforces its strength. This card is a positive card depicting the person's achievements in his lifetime.

The Ten of Pentacles

The Ten of Pentacles is a positive card, indicating a dynasty of assets and wealth. The person is accumulating material possessions, and transferring them to the members of his family.

When both the Nine and Ten of Pentacles appear in certain spreads, this is a sign of the ultimate material success.

King of Pentacles

The King of Pentacles corresponds to the astrological symbol of Capricorn.

When **positive**, this card indicates long-term success in the material sense, stability and economic security.

When the card is **negative**, the meaning involves bureaucracy, pettiness, danger that one's wealth will be confiscated (into the government coffers).

This card is primarily influential for those whose astrological sign is Capricorn and Taurus.

Queen of Pentacles

The Queen of Pentacles corresponds to the astrological symbol of Taurus. It is a combination of wealth and love, as well as subliminal eroticism (as depicted by the rabbit).

When the card is **positive** it indicates stability in all areas of the person's life, but when the card is **negative**, there is a danger of losing one's wealth due to one's desires.

This card is primarily influential for those whose astrological sign is Taurus or Cancer.

Page of Pentacles

The Page of Pentacles corresponds to the astrological symbol of Virgo. The image on the card is familiar to us, one who is searching his way in the material world. The card may be positive or negative, depending on its position within the spread.

When the card is **positive,** the person is diligent, energetic and will succeed.

When the card is **negative**, the person has narrow horizons, is suspicious and does not take any initiative.

This card is primarily influential for those whose astrological sign is Virgo or Pisces.

Swords

Ace (1) of Swords

The Ace of Swords is a positive card. One hand is holding a sword whose colors are blue and white. On the sword there is a crown adorned with the fruits of success, olive and date branches. The person has chosen his path and now he is on his "way up," without stopping to look at the desert beneath him. This is a card that requires the person to make a decision, and guarantees that his decision will be a positive one.

Two of Swords

The Two of Swords is a negative card. The eyes of the figure are blindfolded, and the swords are difficult to balance.

This is a person in a state of apathy due to his inability to decide. It is a very serious card.

Three of Swords

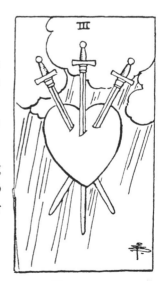

The Three of Swords is a serious card, even disastrous! The heart is torn apart by the swords! There is no base beneath the picture.

It is a difficult card, indicating hard times. The only chance is to wait for the clouds to pass in order to see the sun again.

Four of Swords

The Four of Swords is another card whose interpretation is determined by the spread. Is this the rest of a weary warrior before a battle, or perhaps it is the repose that leads towards eternal death.

Notice the hands of the figure in the card, as well as the open window, and the scene that can be perceived through it. Perhaps through spiritual advice the person can awaken from his slumber?

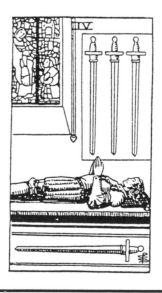

Five of Swords

The Five of Swords is a serious card. The battle is over, but this is a Pyrrhic victory. The warrior remains alone, and now the entire burden is on him.

This person is certain that, since he was triumphant in the battle, he will be able to win the war alone, but this is not the case.

Six of Swords

The Six of Swords is a positive card – it points towards a positive goal, helping the needy, through peaceful action.

Notice that the person rowing the boat has put down all of his swords! This card directs the person to look around him and assist those who are close to him.

Seven of Swords

The Seven of Swords shows us a person wearing a red fez (which indicates that he is sly, because he is a "Muslim" according to Western culture) who is running from a military camp (notice the flags) having stolen all the weapons. This is a serious card, which is sometimes referred to as "the Traitor."

There is one positive thing – this card may be warning the querent of an unexpected betrayal.

Eight of Swords

The Eight of Swords is the card of the captive. The woman is bound and she is surrounded by bars made of eight swords. She must certainly feel like Andromeda chained to the stone.

This card indicates a serious crisis, and only a daring action, preferably with the help of others, can help the person relieve it.

Nine of Swords

The Nine of Swords is a difficult card, which indicates that the person cannot sleep at night, and all of the swords are hanging above his head (like the sword of Damocles).

The card hints that when the morning dawns, the person will be able to stand on his own two feet.

Ten of Swords

The Ten of Swords is a very serious card. It is the end! All of the swords have been stuck in the back of the victim (Betrayal!).

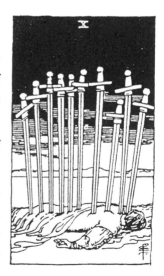

This is the greatest failure of all!

Even the positive cards surrounding it in the spread cannot completely wipe out the serious nature of the card's interpretation.

King of Swords

The King of Swords corresponds to the astrological symbol of Libra. It is the power of control, a sullen king sits on the thrown, bearing his sword prior to making a decision.

The interpretation of the card depends on the other cards near it, which can tip the balance. When the card is **positive,** the person will achieve balance and harmony. When the card is **negative**, this indicates hesitancy that impedes action.

This card is primarily influential for those whose astrological sign is Libra or Gemini.

Queen of Swords

The Queen of Swords corresponds to the astrological symbol of Aquarius. The fact that the figure appears in profile indicates that things are not final, and the querent must decide on his path. When the card is **positive,** the person is capable of making a decision. When the card is **negative**, the person has a narrow perspective.

In any case, the card that is exposed before and after this card has a great deal of influence.

This card is primarily influential for those whose astrological sign is Aquarius or Capricorn.

Page of Swords

The Page of Swords corresponds to the astrological symbol of Gemini. The figure in the card is familiar to us. He is waving his sword, which is only partly visible to us, challenging the unknown.

This card indicates the ability to make a decision and learn from one's experience.

When the card is **positive** – it indicates the ability to "forge ahead" and find the good in everything.

When the card is **negative** – it indicates superficiality, instability, confusion, lack of knowledge.

Knight

The cards of the Knights open new doors before us, and herein lies their importance. They are unique to the tarot cards. [To a certain extent, they are comparable to the jokers in a regular deck of playing cards.]

In principle, all the Knight cards indicate a new path! The precise interpretation depends on the position of the card, as to whether the card is positive or negative.

Knight of Cups

The Knight of Cups indicates new realms in the area of desire and emotion, in other words, what the person wants.

147

Knight of Wands

The Knight of Wands indicates new areas in the realm of creativity or enterprise.

Knight of Pentacles

The Knight of Pentacles indicates new areas in the economic or material world.

Knight of Swords

The Knight of Swords indicates new directions for action in the various areas of the querent's life.

KNIGHT of SWORDS.

The precise interpretations of the Knight cards depend on the general spread of the cards. Each of the four knight cards, when they follow a negative card, are very important, since they can show the way to correct the situation.

THE NUMEROLOGY
OF THE TAROT CARDS

When discussing the cards of the Minor Arcana, we must remember that most of them – 40 out of the 56 cards – are cards with strong numerological significance.

There are four suits of cards, and each of them has cards numbering from 1 to 10. To remind you, the number 10 is meaningless from a numerological analysis point of view, because it is number 1 (1+0=1), and shares the characteristics of number 1.

It is important to remember that numerology developed together with the tarot cards. In the places where the tarot card philosophy was developed, the theory of numerology developed as well.

This numerological interpretation is based on the Pythagorean theorem: "Each number has a power, which is not expressed merely in the form of the number or in a numerical expression. This power stems from an occult connection resulting from the principles of nature expressed in the numbers."

The world is built on numbers, and all phenomenon in the world can be contained within the nine digits.

The most accepted version of the numerology of the tarot cards is that of Cornelius Agrippa, and it appears in his book, "The Philosophy of Occultism" (1533). Tarot card readers used to base their readings on the interpretations found in this book.

Number 1 – goal, destiny, aggression, action, ambition. Like the letter "A," this number is like an arrow, directed at reaching its target.

Number 2 – number of antithesis, which contains the extremes of day and night, and balance through integrating opposites.

Number 3 – symbolized by the triangle, which indicates the past, present and future. The number that "adapts."

Number 4 – stability and perseverance, symbolized by the square, and by the four seasons and the basic elements – fire, water, air and earth. It is a "primitive" number.

Number 5 – adventure, this number "moves" and gains experience. Instability which leads to uncertainty. An unexpected number.

Number 6 – dependency. Harmony with nature. Symbolizes the colors of the rainbow in the sky. This number is incredibly balanced, since it is a combination of 2 and 3, being the product when they are multiplied.

Number 7 – mysterious, enables one to learn and know and penetrate the unknown, the hidden world. Represents the seven ruling planets, the seven musical notes, the seven days of the week. In combines the perfection of the number 6 with the singularity of the number 1, and herein lies its spiritual power.

Number 8 – material success. The square doubled. Can be divided into 4 and 4, or 2-2-2-2, and this is the source of its stability.

Number 9 – "total" success. The symbol of the universe. The largest of the single digits. Since it is 3 X 3, it is endowed with inspiration.

Pythagoras

THE SPREADS

These spreads can be done using only the 56 cards of the Minor Arcana, or you may use all 78 cards of the full tarot deck. The spreads discussed below are the basic and most useful.

The Celtic Cross Spread

Using the Celtic Cross spread is the most common and the simplest method. Select one card from the Minor Arcana – this card is the **Significator** which represents the querent or the person for whom the spread is being laid out. The selection may be done on the basis of the person's astrological sign, and according to his age.

The spread is built around this card.

Swords – Air	Cups – Water
Libra	Cancer
Gemini	Scorpio
Aquarius	Pisces

Wands – Fire	Pentacles – Earth
Aries	Taurus
Leo	Virgo
Sagittarius	Capricorn

For each astrological sign, select a card as follows from the appropriate suit:

For a man under age 40, select the Knight card.

For a man over age 40, select the King card.

For a women under age 40, select the Page card.

For a woman over age 40, select the Queen card.

Thus the significator card for a young man with the sign of Pisces would be the Knight of Cups.

Place the significator card face up on the table. The querent, for whom the reading is being conducted, shuffles the remaining cards in the deck, while they are face down, and cuts them into three equal piles. He then selects one of the three piles, and this is the pile to be used in the reading. The remaining cards from the deck are laid aside and they play no additional function in this reading.

Now you, as the card reader, place the cards down in the following order, while describing out loud what you are doing.

The first card covers the significator card, and you say, "This card covers you."

The second card is laid down across the first two cards, and you say, "This card crosses you."

The third card is placed above the significator, and you say, "This card crowns you."

The fourth card is places underneath the significator, and you say, "This card is beneath you."

The fifth card goes to the right of the significator, and you say, "This card is behind you."

The sixth card goes to the left, and you say, "This card is in front of you."

The remaining cards are placed in a row, from bottom to top, to the right of the other cards.

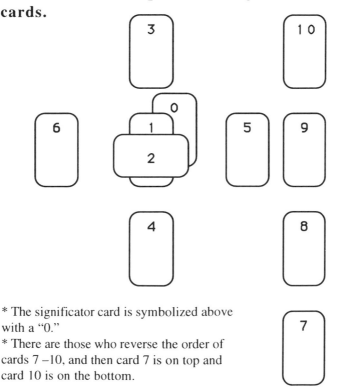

* The significator card is symbolized above with a "0."
* There are those who reverse the order of cards 7 –10, and then card 7 is on top and card 10 is on the bottom.

The seventh card goes at the bottom, and you say, "This is you."

The eight card goes above that, and you say, "This is your home."

The ninth card goes above that, and you say, "These are your hopes and your fears."

The tenth card goes on the top, and you say, "This is your future."

The statements made out loud help both the reader and the querent to concentrate and pay attention to the cards.

After carefully examining the cards before you, relax, breathe deeply, and try to clear your mind of all other thoughts. Look over the cards, and let your gaze wander wherever it will. Then begin by reading the first card, using the list of interpretations described above. But use it flexibly, and use your imagination and intuition to assist you. With time, your extra-sensory ability to absorb the message of the cards will improve, and you may well discover that by using the cards, you will gain true fortune-telling skills.

The Horseshoe Spread

The Horseshoe spread is a simple array, and it is used, in general, to answer a specific question. This spread does not make use of a significator card.

Shuffle the deck of cards and hand them to the querent to shuffle as well, while both of you concentrate on the dilemma being asked about. Take the cards face up, and lay down the top seven cards in a horseshoe shape (see illustration), then read them in a counter-clockwise direction.

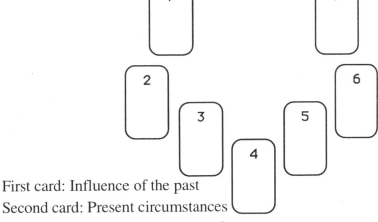

First card: Influence of the past
Second card: Present circumstances
Third card: General trends for the future
Fourth card: The best course of action
Fifth card: Relationships with others
Sixth card: Possible obstacles
Seventh card: Final outcome

Seven-Pointed Star Spread

This spread is sometimes used for the purpose of a weekly forecast.

Place the significator card (see the Celtic Spread) down on the table. Shuffle the rest of the cards and then hand them to the querent. While he holds the deck of cards face down, take seven cards from the top of the deck and place them on the table the way they are shown in the illustration. Now read each of the cards in the following order:

Card 4: Sunday
Card 1: Monday
Card 5: Tuesday
Card 2: Wednesday
Card 6: Thursday
Card 3: Friday
Card 7: Saturday

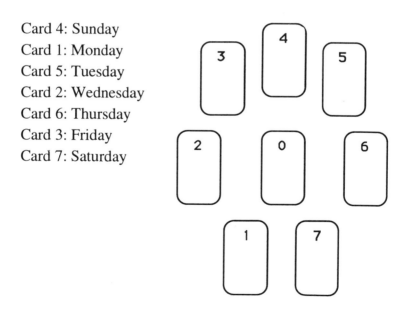

The Circle Spread

This spread can be used to make a year-long forecast. Shuffle the cards, allow the querent to shuffle them a second time, face down.

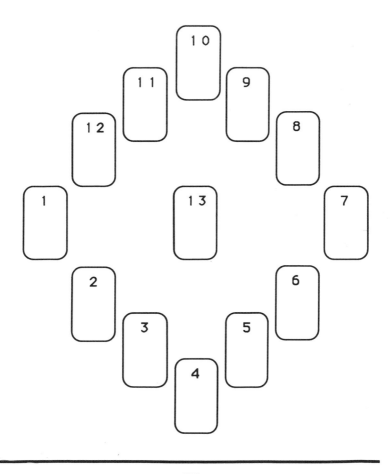

Take 12 cards from the top of the deck and place them on the table face up. The 13th card is placed in the center of the circle; this card dictates the general spirit of the spread, and this card is read first. Then read the rest of the cards one by one, in a counter-clockwise direction.

The first card refers to the coming year in general, the second card indicates events for the second month, the third card signifies events for the third month, etc. beginning from the day the reading takes place and through the end of the year.